MILITARY SPECIAL OPS

MARINE
FORCE RECON

ELITE OPERATIONS

BY MARCIA AMIDON LUSTED

Lerner Publications Company
Minneapolis

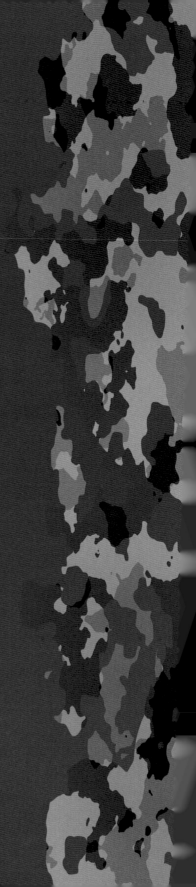

Lerner Publications Company
A division of Lerner Publishing Group, Inc.
241 First Avenue North
Minneapolis, MN 55401 U.S.A.

Website address: www.lernerbooks.com

Content Consultant: Kalev Sepp, assistant professor, Naval Postgraduate School

Library of Congress Cataloging-in-Publication Data

Lusted, Marcia Amidon.
        Marine Force Recon : elite operations / by Marcia Amidon Lusted.
            p.   cm. — (Military special ops)
        Includes index.
        ISBN 978–0–7613–9079–4 (lib. bdg. : alk. paper)
        ISBN 978–1–4677–1765–6 (eBook)
        1. United States. Marine Corps. Force Reconnaissance—Juvenile
    literature. 2. United States. Marine Corps—Commando troops—
    Juvenile literature. I. Title.
    VE23.L89 2014
    359.9'84—dc23   2013002301

Manufactured in the United States of America
1 – MG – 7/15/13

The images in this book are used with the permission of: Ezekiel Kitandwe/ U.S. Marine Corps, 5, 19; Aaron Rooks/U.S. Marine Corps, 6; Mark Stroud/U.S. Marine Corps, 7, 13, 22, 27; U.S. Department of Defense, 9; © AP Images, 10; Alex C. Sauceda/U.S. Marine Corps, 12; U.S. Marine Corps, 15 (top); Chris Stone/U.S. Marine Corps, 15 (bottom); Christopher Nodine/U.S. Navy, 16; Mark Oliva/U.S. Marine Corps, 17; Ali Azimi/U.S. Marine Corps, 21; Matheus Hernandez/U.S. Marine Corps, 23; Matthew Manning/U.S. Marine Corps, 25; Tyler Hill/U.S. Marine Corps, 26; Andrew Avitt/U.S. Marine Corps, 28-29

Front Cover: Lance Cpl. Matthew Manning/U.S. Marines.

Main body text set in Tw Cen MT Std Medium 12/18.
Typeface provided by Adobe Systems

CONTENTS

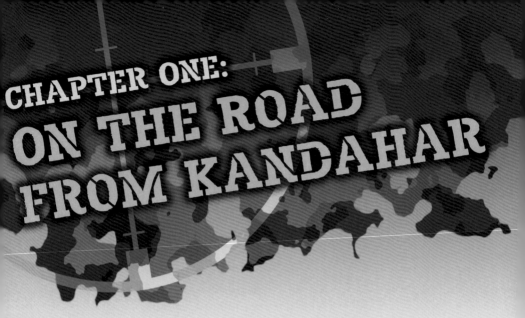

CHAPTER ONE:
ON THE ROAD FROM KANDAHAR

Winter winds churned up storms of pale tan dust. Sometimes it was difficult to see more than a few feet ahead. Anything left exposed, such as radios or weapons, would quickly be ruined. It was December 2001. The United States and its allies were at war in Afghanistan. They were hunting the terrorists responsible for the attacks of September 11, 2001.

Members of the U.S. Marine Corps 1st Force Reconnaissance unit, or 1st Force Recon, watched Highway 1. The road ran between the cities of Kandahar and Lashkar-Gah. Highway 1 was not the best place to lay an ambush. The Marines were in the middle of an open desert plateau. There were no buildings or trees to use for cover.

"The 1st Force Reconnaissance Company Marines . . . were the best-trained, best-equipped Marines fighting in Afghanistan."

—Captain Philip J. Treglia, platoon commander, Marine Force Recon

A Force Recon Marine (*left*) patrols in Afghanistan with an Afghan ally.

The U.S. military was fighting in Kandahar. First Force Recon was one of several U.S. Marine Corps Force Reconnaissance companies. Marine Force Recon units specialize in collecting information behind enemy lines undetected. But that day, 1st Force Recon was operating as a small combat unit. Their mission was to destroy enemy forces escaping from Kandahar.

The team set up a roadblock to stop any vehicles. The Marines were ordered not to use deadly force unless the enemy threatened them. An approaching convoy of enemy trucks attempted to speed around the roadblock. This was considered a hostile act.

Force Recon Marines in Afghanistan await a nighttime pickup by helicopter.

The Marine Force Recon unit surrounded the vehicles. Shooting broke out. A truck from the enemy convoy loaded with ammunition and grenades caught fire. The Marines called in an air strike. Aircraft destroyed the enemy truck and several other vehicles trying to avoid the roadblock.

Marine Force Recon units usually stay out of sight. But 1st Force Recon had the training they needed to ambush the enemy. Their experience helped them realize the convoy was hostile and decide to shoot. When the team returned to camp, two more reconnaissance patrols went out. They sought any enemy fighters who had made it past the roadblock. Other patrols went into nearby villages. They looked for hidden enemy weapons.

The Marines of 1st Force Recon accomplished their mission that day. Marine Force Recon units have three main duties: reconnaissance,

Force Recon Marines practice jungle movement. Units must be able to operate in difficult terrain.

attacks, and special independent missions. Their Afghanistan mission was more visible than most Marine Force Recon operations. They are one of the elite special forces in the military. But they are also one of the least known. Their actions are often so secret that no one even knows they were there.

TECHNOLOGY MALFUNCTION

Marine 1st Force Recon planted several ground sensors in enemy territory in Afghanistan. Ground sensors can record the movement and location of enemy vehicles. The sensors then send activity reports or images back to headquarters. However, these ground sensors did not work well in the loose, powdery desert sand of Afghanistan. The sensors could not record movement from as far away as they usually could. Regardless, the Marines of 1st Force Recon were ready to fight when the enemy appeared.

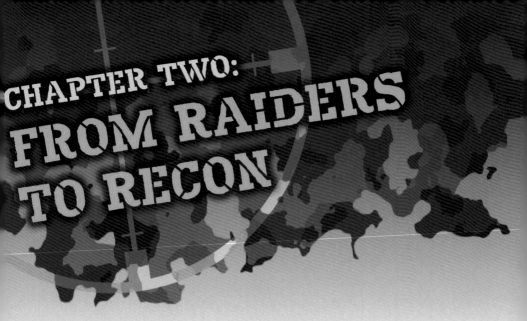

CHAPTER TWO: FROM RAIDERS TO RECON

During the Revolutionary War (1775–1783), the Continental Congress created two companies of Marines. These men usually served on naval ships. They manned the guns and boarded enemy ships. Marines have fought in all U.S. conflicts. They became one of the main fighting forces against Japan during World War II (1939–1945). Marines fighting in the Pacific needed a special unit for quick strikes and high-risk missions. The Marine Raiders were formed for these missions. They became expert at amphibious attacks. They attacked the enemy quickly while larger army and Marine Corps units prepared for bigger battles. Marine Raiders could land anywhere to raid Japanese positions. They needed little time to get ready.

The Marine Raiders only fought from 1942 to 1944. The war in the Pacific changed. The enemy moved into strongly held forts and well-guarded small islands. The Raiders' tactics were not as effective in those situations.

Marine Raiders in the Solomon Islands rally in front of a Japanese hideout they captured.

Force Recon Marines on patrol during the Vietnam War (1957–1975) watch for enemy ambushes.

The Marines still needed a unit for reconnaissance, however. The Amphibious Reconnaissance Company—or Amphib Recon for short—was created for this purpose. These Marines went to small islands occupied by Japanese forces. They gathered information about enemy soldiers, equipment, and forts. They looked for problems that might hold back invading Allied forces.

After World War II, the Amphib Recon companies weren't needed anymore. The units were closed down. They were brought back during the Korean War (1950–1953), however. The first U.S. Marine Corps Force Reconnaissance unit was officially created in 1957. Marine Force Recon played an important role during the Vietnam War. After the war, the size of the U.S. military decreased, including Marine Force Recon. Then, in the 1980s, the military expanded again. Special forces were strengthened as well. Marine Force Recon was given new equipment, better training, and more men. They played an important part in Operation Desert Storm (1990–1991). They served in the conflicts in Iraq (2003–2010) and Afghanistan (2001–present).

MISSION IN FOCUS

KILLER KANE

In 1967 1st Force Recon was operating in Vietnam. One of its teams used the code name "Killer Kane." On July 21, 1967, Killer Kane was doing reconnaissance near the Suoi Ca Valley. They needed to see how many and how strong the enemy was before other Marines went in. The team was stationed on a high ridge. They heard loud voices. They thought there might be other Marines in the area. Instead, it was the Vietcong enemy. Team Killer Kane quickly set up a four-man ambush. The enemy was so surprised they barely fired a shot. After ten minutes of intense fire from the Marines, all was quiet. Team Killer Kane found that most of the enemy had run away rather than stayed to fight. The Marines found many enemy weapons and supplies left on the ground. They also found 40 pounds (18 kilograms) of documents. These included Vietcong codes, troop information, diaries, and equipment lists. It was the largest seizure of weapons and intelligence ever by a recon patrol at that time.

A Force Recon team practices being lifted into a helicopter.

Most special forces units in the military were combined in 1987. They became part of Special Operations Command (SOCOM). But Marine Force Recon did not become part of that organization. Marine Force Recon instead remains under direct command of the Marines.

Marine Force Recon is often the first to arrive on the scene of a conflict. These Marines can fight if they have to. However, their chief role is deep reconnaissance. Deep means they may go far inside enemy territory. They gather as much detailed information as possible.

Force Recon Marines practice diving to approach their targets underwater.

MARINE CORPS FORCES SPECIAL OPERATIONS COMMAND

In 2006 the Marines created the Marine Corps Forces Special Operations Command (MARSOC). MARSOC takes part in special operations. It is under the command of SOCOM. Marine Force Recon is not part of MARSOC, but the two groups sometimes share missions. Marine Force Recon and MARSOC Marines receive similar training and equipment.

They avoid detection. Then other fighting forces follow them into the area. These soldiers use the information gathered during the reconnaissance missions. Without Marine Force Recon units going in first, the forces that follow would have less information in hostile situations. They might not know how many enemy fighters are present or what problems they might face. Within the elite military special forces, Marine Force Recon is respected as one of the best. Their training is intensive and lengthy. Their members are some of the best military men in the world.

CHAPTER THREE: SWIFT, SILENT, AND DEADLY

So what is Marine Force Recon's most important role? The teams gather intelligence and provide it to the rest of the U.S. military. They get this information through reconnaissance. Reconnaissance can be amphibious. This includes activities such as swimming, investigating a coastline or beach, or using small boats. Reconnaissance is also done on foot. Sometimes Marines parachute or fast-rope from an aircraft. Reconnaissance is not the same as spying, however. Spies gather information but do not fight. Marine Force Recon units can fight when they need to. Marine Force Recon roles are grouped into two categories. One role is reconnaissance of any kind. The other is taking direct action such as hostage rescues, raids, strikes, and ambushes.

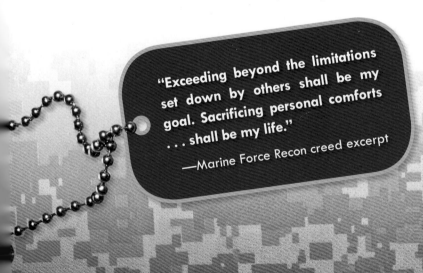

"Exceeding beyond the limitations set down by others shall be my goal. Sacrificing personal comforts . . . shall be my life."

—Marine Force Recon creed excerpt

Force Recon Marines use many techniques to gather intelligence.

A Marine Force Recon candidate trains for direct action missions.

Marines in Zodiac boats approach the *Magellan Star* to rescue its crew.

Marine Force Recon members have other jobs as well. They fight pirates who attack friendly oceangoing ships. In 2010 a Force Recon unit came to the aid of *Magellan Star*, a German tanker. Pirates had boarded the tanker south of Yemen in the Indian Ocean. The Force Recon unit approached the captured vessel in Zodiac rubber boats. The Marines boarded the ship and fought their way to the bridge. They captured some of the pirates and chased those who tried to escape. Eleven crew members were rescued.

Marine Force Recon units also perform search and seizure. They enter an enemy ship or camp secretly. They look for illegal or sensitive objects or documents and take them. They might also have to fight an enemy force. Force Recon Marines were part of Operation Praying Mantis in the Persian Gulf in 1988. They did a search and seizure on an oil platform. Iranian forces were rumored to be hiding there, threatening U.S. troops. A Force Recon team attacked the platform, located the enemy, and took out the threat.

A Force Recon Marine searches an Iraqi home for enemy plans.

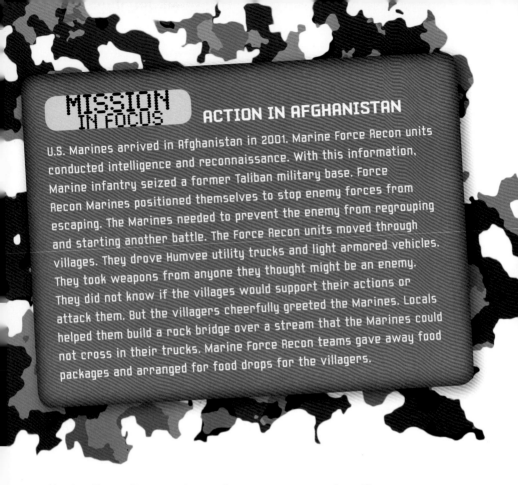

U.S. Marines arrived in Afghanistan in 2001. Marine Force Recon units conducted intelligence and reconnaissance. With this information, Marine infantry seized a former Taliban military base. Force Recon Marines positioned themselves to stop enemy forces from escaping. The Marines needed to prevent the enemy from regrouping and starting another battle. The Force Recon units moved through villages. They drove Humvee utility trucks and light armored vehicles. They took weapons from anyone they thought might be an enemy. They did not know if the villages would support their actions or attack them. But the villagers cheerfully greeted the Marines. Locals helped them build a rock bridge over a stream that the Marines could not cross in their trucks. Marine Force Recon teams gave away food packages and arranged for food drops for the villagers.

Marine Force Recon units perform counterterrorism. They rescue hostages. They launch small surprise raids to support other Marine forces. They also provide security for military or government leaders. This is called a personal security detail.

A basic Marine Force Recon unit is a team of three to five men. Their leader is a staff sergeant. Next in rank is an assistant leader. The team also includes three scouts and one radio operator. Four or five of these teams together make up a platoon. A platoon usually has about twenty men. A lieutenant or a captain leads a platoon. Six platoons make up a company, led by a captain or a major. Each company has its own specially trained units in charge of intelligence, communications, and supplies. Each Marine Force Recon company operates in specific area of the world. There are approximately two thousand Force Recon Marines in all.

A Force Recon Marine maintains friendly ties with locals in Afghanistan.

CHAPTER FOUR: GEARING UP

Marine Force Recon units perform many types of missions, so the Marines need many types of equipment. Force Recon Marines wear different uniforms depending on their location and mission. During ground operations, Marines wear vests that hold weapons and equipment. They wear camouflage-patterned pants, shirts, and jackets. The camouflage varies to match their surroundings. They wear black or brown jungle boots. They generally wear standard body armor and helmets for protection.

Marines sometimes wear Full Spectrum Battle Equipment (FSBE) in combat. It includes body armor vests with pockets for ammunition magazines. Helmets have built-in communications systems and also float. FSBE also includes a breathing device with one to two minutes of air and a flotation collar. For other missions, Marines might wear Nomex bodysuits. Nomex is a light, fire-resistant fabric. It helps protect Marines from explosions. The suit comes with Nomex gloves, a Nomex head and face covering called a balaclava, and goggles.

Marine Force Recon weapons include a standard M4 rifle. Marines also carry shotguns and MP5 submachine guns. The types of weapons used depend on the mission. Marines usually carry knives as well.

"I could speak for days about these great men. They are absolutely fearless."
—Lieutenant Colonel George W. Smith Jr., former commanding officer of 1st Force Recon

A Force Recon Marine wears a uniform that protects and camouflages him.

Other equipment aids Marines in reconnaissance missions. They use satellite radios to communicate. Observation telescopes, computer digital photo systems, GPS, and night-vision binoculars help them gather intelligence. Thermal imaging cameras detect objects at night by the heat they put out. Laser markers pinpoint locations for airplanes to bomb targets or pick up Marines.

THERMAL IMAGERS

Marine Force Recon units use thermal imagers for surveillance. A long-range thermal imager is a combination of camera and binoculars. It scans heat put out by objects within its view. It can be used by hand or remote control. The imager helps the soldiers see people and things at night or in smoke, fog, rain, or dust. The display quality is almost as good as a regular television image.

The Diver Propulsion Device can pull two Marines and their equipment quickly underwater to their targets.

Transportation options include Humvees, dune buggies, and several types of inflatable rafts and boats. The dune buggies can carry a three-man crew as well as weapons. They are mostly used for transportation, not fighting. Force Recon Marines are trained to use parachutes. In high-altitude, low-opening (HALO) jumps, they free fall until they are close to the ground before opening their parachutes. This makes it harder for enemies to spot the Marines. HALO jumps require a special helmet, flight suit, and boots.

For scouting coastlines, Marines might need wetsuits. Scuba gear allows them to operate underwater unseen. They use special underwater breathing systems that do not leave a trail of bubbles.

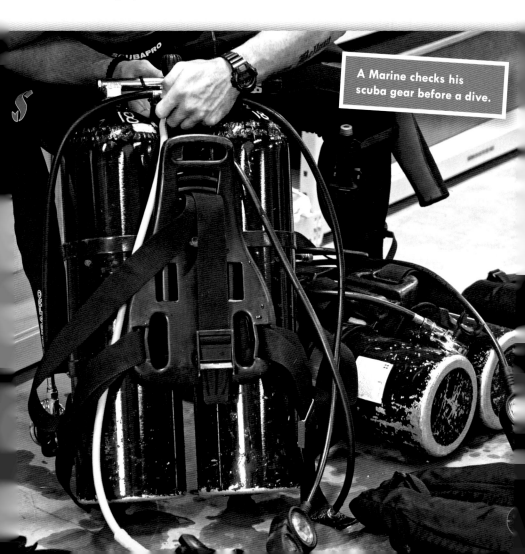

A Marine checks his scuba gear before a dive.

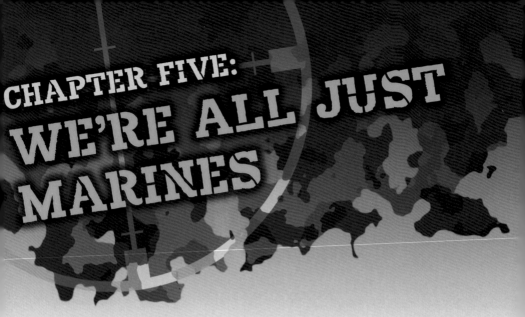

CHAPTER FIVE: WE'RE ALL JUST MARINES

Marine Force Recon members have special training and skills, but they don't consider themselves better than other Marines. It takes many years of extremely difficult training to become a member of Marine Force Recon. No women have yet served in Marine Force Recon. A candidate first has to serve in the Marines for three to five years. The candidate must have an excellent performance record. He must hold the rank of corporal or higher.

Candidates have to pass a physical test. This includes sit-ups, pull-ups, an obstacle course, and a 3-mile (4.8-kilometer) timed run wearing a loaded pack. Candidates might be asked to do any part of the test over again at any time. The candidates jump into a swimming pool wearing their uniforms, including their boots. They must swim 500 yards (457 meters) in seventeen minutes. Then they have to tread water for one minute while holding their rifles. Then, without any rest, they put on 50-pound (23 kg) packs and march for two and a half hours. These tests are designed to be very difficult. Only the best applicants will be accepted into training.

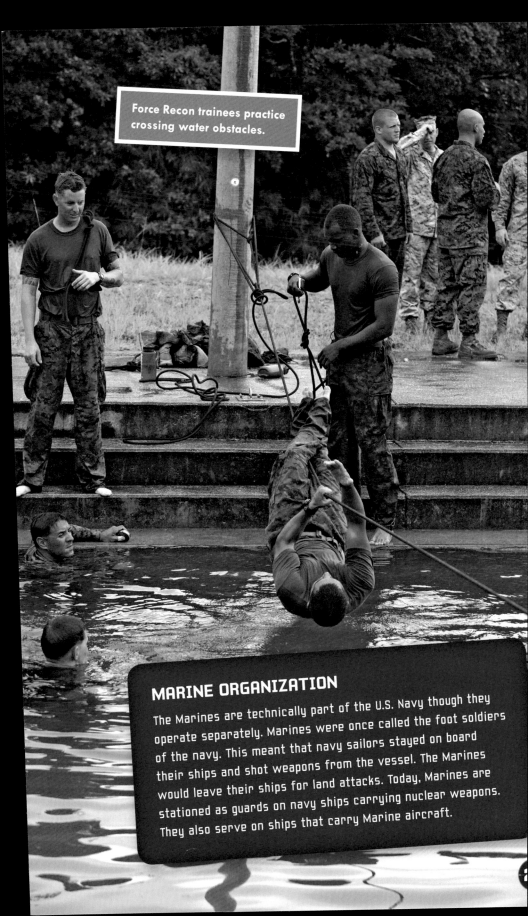

Force Recon trainees practice crossing water obstacles.

MARINE ORGANIZATION

The Marines are technically part of the U.S. Navy though they operate separately. Marines were once called the foot soldiers of the navy. This meant that navy sailors stayed on board their ships and shot weapons from the vessel. The Marines would leave their ships for land attacks. Today, Marines are stationed as guards on navy ships carrying nuclear weapons. They also serve on ships that carry Marine aircraft.

Marines practice free-fall parachuting.

Once the physical test is over, candidates take a written exam to test their intelligence. Then a group of Force Recon veterans interviews them. The interview determines who has the right attitude to join. Only 20 percent of applicants make it into training.

Training takes six months. The Marines use training facilities from other branches of the military. Trainees attend the U.S. Army Airborne School and the Marine Corps Mountain Warfare Training Center. They go to the U.S. Navy Combat Diving School and Survival, Evasion, Resistance, and Escape (SERE) school. At SERE school, they learn what to do if they are captured and how to escape. Some candidates also go through the U.S. Army Ranger School.

Throughout their training, Force Recon candidates acquire many skills. They learn patrolling and reconnaissance. They practice winter survival, rock climbing, pathfinding, and basic medical skills. They are trained in many different types of radio and satellite communication. They learn how to enter and leave submarines underwater. They fast-rope from helicopters. They practice parachuting from aircrafts at different heights. They also get extensive training in weapons. They learn to identify and fire weapons from other countries. They practice demolition with explosives. They study techniques for rescuing hostages.

Force Recon Marines use inflatable Zodiac boats.

> **"Nah, we're all just Marines."**
> —Force Recon member, after being asked if there was any envy between them and regular Marines

At the end of training, Marine Force Recon trainees face a final field exercise. The exercise makes them combine everything they have learned. They attack a location from the water. They must then rescue a pretend hostage. The exercise also includes a parachute jump and mountain and desert patrols. Finally, Marines must measure and describe a beach or a harbor for features that might affect battle operations. Once they've passed these tests, candidates are assigned to Marine Force Recon units around the world. They are ready for real

Force Recon Marines practice securing a beach so they can survey it.

missions, including hostage rescues and dealing with pirates. Finally, they officially become Marine Force Recon members.

Even after so much special training, the average Force Recon Marine only stays in the unit for five years. Then he returns to the regular Marine Corps. The special skills and knowledge these Marines have gained benefit everyone in the Corps.

GLOSSARY

ALLIES
friendly nations that often help one another in wars

AMBUSH
surprise attack from a hidden position

AMPHIBIOUS
taking place by land and sea

CAMOUFLAGE
disguising military equipment or people by covering or painting them so that they blend in with their surroundings

COUNTERTERRORISM
political or military activities designed to stop terrorism

DEMOLITION
in the military, destruction of something that weakens the enemy

FAST-ROPE
technique used to slide down a rope from a helicopter

INTELLIGENCE
information of military or political value

RECONNAISSANCE
secret information gathering

SURVEILLANCE
keeping a close watch on something

TALIBAN
militant Islamic movement of Pashtun tribesmen from around Afghanistan

THERMAL
having to do with heat

Further Reading

Gordon, Nick. *Marine Corps Force Recon*. Minneapolis: Bellwether Media, 2013.

Loria, Laura. *Marine Force Recon*. Milwaukee: Gareth Stevens Publishing, 2012.

Lusted, Marcia Amidon. *Army Delta Force: Elite Operations*. Minneapolis: Lerner Publications Company, 2014.

Sandler, Michael. *Marine Force Recon in Action*. New York: Bearport Publishing, 2008.

Websites

American Special Ops: Marine Force Recon
http://forcerecon.americanspecialops.com/
This website includes information on what Force Recon is and what types of training and missions its Marines accomplish.

How Stuff Works: How the US Marines Work
http://www.howstuffworks.com/marines.htm
This website features information on the history and purpose of the Marine Corps.

U.S. Marine Corps
http://www.marines.mil/
The official website of the U.S. Marine Corps highlights news, history, information, and photos.

INDEX

About the Author

Marcia Amidon Lusted has written more than seventy-five books and 350 magazine articles for young readers. She is also a magazine editor, a writing instructor, and a musician.